W9-ANN-408

OIL, COAL AND GAS

FROM THIS EARTH

William Russell

The Rourke Corporation, Inc.
Vero Beach, Florida 32964

PHOTO CREDITS
Courtesy American Petroleum Institute: cover, title page, pages 4,
7, 12, 13, 17, 18, 21
Courtesy Illinois Department of Minerals and Mines: pages 8, 10
Courtesy Northern Illinois Gas Company: page 15

Library of Congress Cataloging-in-Publication Data

Russell, William, 1942–
    Oil, coal and gas / by William Russell.
        p. cm. — (From this earth)
    Includes index.
    ISBN 0-86593-357-X
    1. Fossil fuels—Juvenile literature. [1. Fossil fuels.]
I. Title II. Series.
TP318.R87 1994
662'.6—dc20
                                        94-2401
                                        CIP
Printed in the USA   AC

TABLE OF CONTENTS

OIL

Oil is a dark, syrupy liquid most often found in deep, underground pools. Oil, or petroleum, is an important source of fuel.

Scientists believe that the underground pools of oil came from billions of bodies of **ancient**—very old—sea plants and animals. During the passage of millions of years, the bodies were squeezed under tremendous weight. Above them were mud, sand, water and rock.

The weight and other natural forces turned these tiny plants and animal bodies into oil and natural gas.

Drilling rigs along the seacoasts take oil from pools in the layers of rock beneath the sea

NATURAL GAS

Like the air we breathe, natural gas is invisible. It cannot be poured, felt or forced into a shape. But it can be collected, transported and burned. Like oil, natural gas is an important fuel. **Gasoline** is a liquid fuel made from oil.

Nature has been producing natural gas underground for millions of years. It is often found with oil deposits.

A natural gas drilling rig stands against a fiery sunset in Texas

COAL

We know coal as a dark, shiny rock used for fuel. Curiously, coal came from soft, green plants that grew in swamps and died millions of years ago.

The plants rotted into soft material called **peat**. Under the great weight of rock and mud and water for millions of years, the peat hardened into coal. Some coal **beds**, or deposits, are deeper than a football field is long.

FINDING FOSSIL FUELS

Natural gas, coal and petroleum are **fossil** fuels. Fossils are the remains of ancient plants and animals.

The scientists who study the earth and its rocks look for fossil fuels only in certain places. Oil and natural gas are usually found where there were seas or where there are seas today. And scientists limit their hunt to those parts of the seas with certain kinds of bottoms.

Scientists look for fossil fuels, like coal, only in certain areas

A diver welds an underwater pipeline

Operators at a refinery adjust insulation on a heating machine

LANDS OF FOSSIL FUELS

The United States is the world's largest user of petroleum and the world's second largest **producer** of petroleum. But most of the world's known petroleum pools, called **reserves**, are in the Middle East. Saudi Arabia itself has one-fourth of the known oil reserves.

In North America, Texas, Alaska, Alberta, California and Louisiana are the leading oil producers. The leading coal producers are Wyoming, Kentucky, West Virginia, Pennsylvania and Illinois.

A natural gas pipeline snakes across Texas

MINING FOSSIL FUELS

Coal is usually removed from the ground by strip mining. The soil is stripped, or taken, away from above a bed of coal. Then the coal is dug out after it has been broken up by dynamite.

Oil and natural gas are located by huge drills plunged into the earth. Oil and natural gas are removed by pipes.

Strip, or surface, mining for coal in Wyoming

USING FOSSIL FUELS

Fossil fuels burn easily. As they burn, they release heat. Heat can be changed into power. Much of the electric power in North America comes from fossil fuels. Almost all the cars, trains, ships and aircraft are powered by fossil fuels. Many factories also run on fossil fuels.

Oil from the ground—petroleum—can be **refined**, or changed, into several fuels with special uses. Gasoline, kerosene, diesel fuel and engine oil are all products from petroleum.

Like other fossil fuels, coal burns easily and produces heat and energy

PROBLEMS WITH FOSSIL FUELS

The world's richest nations use tremendous amounts of fossil fuel. The fuel provides many good things—warm homes, useful products, and swift, comfortable transportation. But fossil fuels also cause problems.

The burning of fossil fuels releases certain poisons that **pollute**, or dirty, the air and water. Another problem for the United States is the need to buy oil from other countries. That sends huge amounts of American dollars overseas.

Scientists look for ways to make fossil fuels burn more cleanly and with less waste

SAVING FOSSIL FUELS

Using fossil fuels for energy has become a way of life for nearly everyone in North America. Trouble is, nature takes millions of years to produce oil, natural gas and coal. People are using these fossil fuels much faster than nature replaces them.

No one knows how long the Earth's fossil fuels will last. But the reserves are limited. Meanwhile, scientists are searching for new fuels to take their place.

Glossary

ancient (AIN chent) — very old

bed (BED) — a layer or deposit of materials such as coal

fossil (FAH suhl) — the ancient remains of plants and animals

gasoline (GAHS uh leen) — a liquid made from petroleum and used as a fuel

peat (PEET) — a stage of plant decay which occurs with certain plants in some wet conditions

pollute (puh LOOT) — to make something dirty or poisonous

producer (pro DO sir) — someone or something that creates a product

refine (reh FINE) — to process a substance in such a way that it is changed into other useful substances

reserve (reh ZERV) — an unused deposit of oil, natural gas or coal

INDEX